I0111148

Training With A Purpose

Shennette Sparkes

Divine Legacy Publishing

Published by Divine Legacy Publishing

Copyright © 2016 by Shennette Sparkes

ISBN 978 0 692 82798 7

All rights reserved. No part of this publication may be reproduced, distributed, or transmitted in any form or by any means, including photocopying, recording, or other electronic or mechanical methods, without the prior written permission of the publisher, except in the case of brief quotations embodied in critical reviews and certain other noncommercial uses permitted by copyright law. For permission requests, write to the publisher, addressed "Attention: Permissions Publisher," at the following address: DivineLegacyPublishing.com

Author Contact:
Shennette Sparkes
higherlearninghoops.com

Cover Image: iStock
Cover Design: Natalie Castillo - ByNatalieCastillo.com

Foreword

Shennette Sparkes is not just an average woman.

A definition of average, according to the Merriam-Webster dictionary, is the level that is typical of a group. Qualities that a plethora of people contain or have are also seen as average or typical. The one who is able to achieve things above and beyond average is then described as extraordinary. Shennette's qualities are undeniably extraordinary. Her qualities and will power are undeniably God given, not only because of her essential purpose in people's lives, but also her consistent efforts to help people around her. These qualities that she possesses have provided her with the strength and confidence to impact everyone she encounters.

Shennette was raised in Fort Lauderdale, Florida where she attended St. Thomas Aquinas High School. She earned varsity letters in three sports: volleyball, basketball, and track. Achieving many things through out her high school career and also being nominated as a McDonalds All American in 2006, Shennette was a beast in every area. She received college scholarship offers in all of her chosen sports, but she chose to further her career playing basketball. She then chose to attend the University of North Florida (UNF) in Jacksonville, Florida on a basketball scholarship playing under Coach Tappmeyer from 2006-2010. She also received the Florida Bright Futures scholarship and extra scholarship money that greatly showed Shennette's ability to be successful on and off the court.

When playing basketball at UNF, Shennette was diagnosed with a chronic illness called Lupus. She was diagnosed with two types of Lupus, but that did not stop her from achieving greatness at UNF. She completed her four years at UNF and then went to play semi-professional for the Orlando Extreme. Her Lupus then began to flare up, which required her to take a step back from actively playing basketball. But, Shennette could never neglect her love for the game of basketball and as time went by, she began coaching. She went from coaching girls to boys, to women to men, from all ages groups. Shennette has taken her talents and coached in middle school, high school, college, and professional basketball arenas.

By sharing her knowledge of basketball with people, she was also able to share her testimony. Shennette speaks all over the state of Florida and will soon be speaking all over the world. She uses her life story as her platform when speaking out to people of all ages. Motivation is an essential aspect of Shennette's character. She may be seen as a motivational speaker, but Shennette could be described as many things. Most importantly, she is relentless. She has allowed people around her to witness the blessings that come with having an unbreakable relationship with Jesus Christ. With God's assistance, she was able to overcome things that were seen as impossible by others. She has been allowed to be viewed as the most influential role model a woman or even a girl could have.

Shennette Sparkes is a woman of many words and knowledge. Reading a book from her will not only allow you to recognize your worth, but you will also learn to use it to your advantage.

- Shakarri Mack

Introduction

My name is Shennette Sparkes. I am wife, mother, coach, mentor, youth leader, and educator. In life we are faced with many challenges. Whether it's family problems, your social income status, or a devastating illness I have learned that the way we respond and allow these circumstances to define us makes the ultimate difference in our life. I grew up in Ft. Lauderdale Florida off of Sistrunk blvd. Mr. Sistrunk was the First African American to own a business in Ft. Lauderdale. He made it possible for other blacks to own property, earn educations, and gain wealth. However, over 30 years later only 2% of African American girls in Ft. Lauderdale obtained a college degree. In the 1990s there was a large increase in teen pregnancy which lasted until 2001 according to the Florida Department of Health.

As a girl growing up in Ft. Lauderdale, I loved my city. If you watched the national news all they talked about was the famous war on drugs and the AIDS epidemic that was plaguing our streets. My brothers and I were blessed to be put in places like our local church, the Boys and Girls, and the Urban League while our parents worked that insured we grew up with structure. The good old village to raise a child mentality really helped to shape me in to the person I am today. Being a Girl Scout forced me to be creative, being an athlete helped me develop mental toughness, being a student gave me knowledge and power, being an older sister made me a leader, being a Christian allowed me to be a servant, and being a leader taught me the value of discipline.

Through out my life I have faced several challenges, from being sexually molested as a young girl, to living homeless in my mother's car in middle school, to overcoming 8 years of battling the chronic illness Lupus. With each challenge, I was able to learn something new, gain strength, and develop my faith. My favorite scripture as a kid was Philippians 4:13: "I can do all things through Christ who strengthens me". This scripture soon became my life's motto. Understanding that in life things happen is important, like the famous questions askes "Why does bad things happen to good people?" For me, my goal wasn't to find out why these things happened to me, but how I can use these situations to help myself and others no longer suffer silently. We have to stay motivated mentally and engaged spiritually to survive.

I composed a book of quotes that have motivated me and inspired me in my life. Some of these quotes are from famous athletes, educators, politicians, and authors. Other quotes are from my mother, Dr. Rosalind Osgood, and my good friend Amy Dobrikova. The last selection of quotes is written be me. I travel the world as a Christian Youth Leader, Basketball Coach and Motivational Sspeaker, which has given me the opportunity to talk to 3,000 athletes, coaches, parents and educators about developing the heart of a champion. The only way we can truly overcome life difficulties, is to understand that life is a process in which we are constantly growing and being molded for the next step. #TrainingWithAPurpose helps us focus on the passion and strength inside of us that allows us to persevere to the end. Whether your next step is high school or college, the military or owning your own business, life's champions always train on purpose. Many of the same principles like self-discipline, and persistence I learned as a basketball player became essential to overcome my battle with Lupus.

Each quote represents different traits of a champion and someone who is training on purpose. After reading each quote, take some time to write about how the quote relates to you and your life.

- Shennette Sparkes

Training With A Purpose

journal

PERSISTENCE

*"Challenges breed champions. We are not defined by
our situation but how we react to these situations."*
                                              - Shennette Sparkes

How does this quote apply to your *life*?

_____

_____

_____

_____

_____

_____

What will you do this week to show **persistence**?

_____

_____

_____

_____

_____

_____

Who do you know that shows **persistence**?

_____

_____

_____

_____

_____

_____

What positive things could come from showing **persistence**?

_____

_____

_____

_____

_____

_____

SELF-DISCIPLINE

"Discipline is what we are willing to do when no one is watching. Great people live a disciplined lifestyle."
- Shennette Sparkes

How does this quote apply to your *life*?

_____
_____
_____
_____
_____
_____

What will you do this week to show *self-discipline*?

_____
_____
_____
_____
_____
_____

Who do you know that shows *self-discipline*?

_____
_____
_____
_____
_____
_____

What positive things could come from showing *self-discipline*?

_____
_____
_____
_____
_____
_____

MENTAL TOUGHNESS

"Only the strong will survive."
- Shennette Sparkes

How does this quote apply to your *life*?

_____
_____
_____
_____
_____
_____

What will you do this week to show *mental toughness*?

_____
_____
_____
_____
_____
_____

Who do you know that shows *mental toughness*?

_____
_____
_____
_____
_____
_____

What positive things could come from showing *mental toughness*?

_____
_____
_____
_____
_____
_____

ENDURANCE

"No one but me!, No matter the highs or lows, no matter which way the wind blows. No matter how hard the glue sticks, no matter how hard the devil kicks, it's me and I will be who I am destined to be!"

- Shennette Sparkes

How does this quote apply to your *life*?

_____
_____
_____
_____
_____

What will you do this week to show *endurance*?

_____
_____
_____
_____
_____

Who do you know that shows *endurance*?

_____
_____
_____
_____
_____

What positive things could come from showing *endurance*?

_____
_____
_____
_____
_____

FOCUS

"Trust in your path! We all are created for our own purpose."
- Shennette Sparkes

How does this quote apply to your _life_?

_____
_____
_____
_____
_____
_____

What will you do this week to show _focus_?

_____
_____
_____
_____
_____
_____

Who do you know that shows _focus_?

_____
_____
_____
_____
_____
_____

What positive things could come from showing _focus_?

_____
_____
_____
_____
_____
_____

#TrainingWithAPurpose | Week 5

PEACE

"The sun may beam the pain of life, while the moon can calm the heart to rest."

- Shennette Sparkes

How does this quote apply to your *life*?

_____

_____

_____

_____

_____

What will you do this week to find *peace*?

_____

_____

_____

_____

_____

Who do you know that is at *peace*?

_____

_____

_____

_____

_____

What positive things could come from finding *peace*?

_____

_____

_____

_____

_____

FAITH

"Champions know they will succeed because they have spent the time investing in their victory!"
- Shennette Sparkes

How does this quote apply to your *life*?

_____

_____

_____

_____

_____

_____

What will you do this week to show *faith*?

_____

_____

_____

_____

_____

_____

Who do you know that has *faith*?

_____

_____

_____

_____

_____

_____

What positive things could come from having *faith*?

_____

_____

_____

_____

_____

_____

PURPOSE

"God allows our character to be developed through the challenges we face and the adversity we have overcome."
- Shennette Sparkes

How does this quote apply to your *life*?

_____
_____
_____
_____
_____

What will you do this week to fulfill your **purpose**?

_____
_____
_____
_____
_____

Who do you know that shows **purpose**?

_____
_____
_____
_____
_____

What positive things could come from following your **purpose**?

_____
_____
_____
_____
_____

CHANGE

"Change allows opportunity for growth."
- Shennette Sparkes

How does this quote apply to your *life*?

_____

_____

_____

_____

_____

What will you do this week to make a *change*?

_____

_____

_____

_____

_____

Who do you know that has made a positive *change*?

_____

_____

_____

_____

_____

What positive things could come from making a *change*?

_____

_____

_____

_____

_____

SELF-CONFIDENCE

"There is nothing wrong with being different. Differences make us unique. What good is putting together a puzzle where all the pieces are exactly the same."

- Shennette Sparkes

How does this quote apply to your *life*?

_____

_____

_____

_____

_____

_____

What will you do this week to show *self-confidence*?

_____

_____

_____

_____

_____

_____

Who do you know that has *self-confidence*?

_____

_____

_____

_____

_____

What positive things could come from having *self-confidence*?

_____

_____

_____

_____

_____

PERSONAL DEVELOPMENT

"Believe in your strength and invest in your weaknesses."
- Shennette Sparkes

How does this quote apply to your *life*?

_____
_____
_____
_____
_____
_____

What will you do this week to **develop**?

_____
_____
_____
_____
_____
_____

Who do you know that has made a positive **development**?

_____
_____
_____
_____
_____
_____

What positive things could come from **developing** as a person?

_____
_____
_____
_____
_____
_____

COURAGE

"Courage isn't about what you will do when no one is looking but what you do when all eyes are on you."
- Shennette Sparkes

How does this quote apply to your *life*?

_____
_____
_____
_____
_____
_____

What will you do this week to *courage*?

_____
_____
_____
_____
_____
_____

Who do you know that shows *courage*?

_____
_____
_____
_____
_____
_____

What positive things could come from having *courage*?

_____
_____
_____
_____
_____

DEDICATION

"Nothing in life happens by chance. We must put in the work daily to turn our dreams into reality."
- Shennette Sparkes

How does this quote apply to your *life*?

_____

_____

_____

_____

_____

_____

What will you do this week to show **dedication**?

_____

_____

_____

_____

_____

_____

Who do you know that shows **dedication**?

_____

_____

_____

_____

_____

What positive things could come from showing **dedication**?

_____

_____

_____

_____

_____

WISDOM

"True champions learn how to overcome adversity."
- Shennette Sparkes

How does this quote apply to your *life*?

_____
_____
_____
_____
_____

What will you do this week to show **wisdom**?

_____
_____
_____
_____
_____

Who do you know that is **wise**?

_____
_____
_____
_____
_____

What positive things could come from **wisdom**?

_____
_____
_____
_____
_____

HOPE

"Never limit yourself, never be satisfied, and smile. It's free!"
- Jennie Finch

How does this quote apply to your *life*?

_____

_____

_____

_____

_____

What will you do this week to show *hope*?

_____

_____

_____

_____

_____

Who do you know that shows *hope*?

_____

_____

_____

_____

_____

What positive things could come from having *hope*?

_____

_____

_____

_____

_____

RESILIENCE

"A successful man is one who can lay a firm foundation with bricks others have thrown at him"

- David Brinkley

How does this quote apply to your *life*?

_____
_____
_____
_____
_____
_____

What will you do this week to show *resilience*?

_____
_____
_____
_____
_____
_____

Who do you know that shows *resilience*?

_____
_____
_____
_____
_____
_____

What positive things could come from being *resilient*?

_____
_____
_____
_____
_____

ATTITUDE

"Your attitude will impact your altitude."
- Shennette Sparkes

How does this quote apply to your *life*?

_____
_____
_____
_____
_____
_____

What will you do this week to have a positive *attitude*?

_____
_____
_____
_____
_____
_____

Who do you know that has a positive *attitude*?

_____
_____
_____
_____
_____
_____

What positive things could come from having a positive *attitude*?

_____
_____
_____
_____
_____
_____

PERSISTENCE

"Keep it moving."

- Shennette Sparkes

How does this quote apply to your *life*?

_____
_____
_____
_____
_____
_____

What will you do this week to show *persistence*?

_____
_____
_____
_____
_____
_____

Who do you know that shows *persistence*?

_____
_____
_____
_____
_____
_____

What positive things could come from showing *persistence*?

_____
_____
_____
_____
_____
_____

SELF-DISCIPLINE

"A smart warrior teaches themselves how to battle before they even reach a war!"

- Shennette Sparkes

How does this quote apply to your *life*?

_____

_____

_____

_____

_____

_____

What will you do this week to show *self-discipline*?

_____

_____

_____

_____

_____

Who do you know that shows *self-discipline*?

_____

_____

_____

_____

_____

What positive things could come from showing *self-discipline*?

_____

_____

_____

_____

_____

MENTAL TOUGHNESS

"The difference between a champion and other people is not what makes them, but what breaks them."
- Shennette Sparkes

How does this quote apply to your *life*?

_____
_____
_____
_____
_____

What will you do this week to show *mental toughness*?

_____
_____
_____
_____
_____

Who do you know that shows *mental toughness*?

_____
_____
_____
_____
_____

What positive things could come from showing *mental toughness*?

_____
_____
_____
_____
_____

ENDURANCE

"Failure shouldn't break you, it should help shape you."
- Shennette Sparkes

How does this quote apply to your *life*?

_____
_____
_____
_____
_____
_____

What will you do this week to show **endurance**?

_____
_____
_____
_____
_____
_____

Who do you know that shows **endurance**?

_____
_____
_____
_____
_____
_____

What positive things could come from showing **endurance**?

_____
_____
_____
_____
_____
_____

FOCUS

"Optimize outstanding opportunities."
- Dr. Rosalind Osgood

How does this quote apply to your *life*?

_____
_____
_____
_____
_____
_____

What will you do this week to show *focus*?

_____
_____
_____
_____
_____
_____

Who do you know that shows *focus*?

_____
_____
_____
_____
_____

What positive things could come from showing *focus*?

_____
_____
_____
_____
_____

PEACE

"Darkness cannot drive out darkness only light can do that.
Hate cannot drive out hate: only love can do that."
                                                    - Martin Luther King Jr.

How does this quote apply to your *life*?

_____

_____

_____

_____

_____

_____

What will you do this week to find **peace**?

_____

_____

_____

_____

_____

_____

Who do you know that is at **peace**?

_____

_____

_____

_____

_____

_____

What positive things could come from finding **peace**?

_____

_____

_____

_____

_____

_____

FAITH

"You will never conquer a fear if you are not willing to face it."
- Shennette Sparkes

How does this quote apply to your *life*?

_____

_____

_____

_____

_____

_____

What will you do this week to show *faith*?

_____

_____

_____

_____

_____

_____

Who do you know that has *faith*?

_____

_____

_____

_____

_____

_____

What positive things could come from having *faith*?

_____

_____

_____

_____

_____

_____

PURPOSE

"We are all born to fly, but it is up to us how high."
- Shennette Sparkes

How does this quote apply to your *life*?

_____
_____
_____
_____
_____
_____

What will you do this week to fulfill your *purpose*?

_____
_____
_____
_____
_____
_____

Who do you know that shows *purpose*?

_____
_____
_____
_____
_____
_____

What positive things could come from following your *purpose*?

_____
_____
_____
_____
_____
_____

CHANGE

"In order to help change the next generation, we must be the change we wish to see."

- Gandhi

How does this quote apply to your *life*?

_____
_____
_____
_____
_____

What will you do this week to make a *change*?

_____
_____
_____
_____
_____

Who do you know that has made a positive *change*?

_____
_____
_____
_____
_____

What positive things could come from making a *change*?

_____
_____
_____
_____
_____

SELF-CONFIDENCE

*"The essence of true beauty lies in what you
see within yourself."*

- Shennette Sparkes

How does this quote apply to your *life*?

_____
_____
_____
_____
_____

What will you do this week to show **self-confidence**?

_____
_____
_____
_____
_____

Who do you know that has **self-confidence**?

_____
_____
_____
_____
_____

What positive things could come from having **self-confidence**?

_____
_____
_____
_____
_____

PERSONAL DEVELOPMENT

"Knowledge is power. The more you learn, the more you are able to accomplish in life."

- Shennette Sparkes

How does this quote apply to your *life*?

_____

_____

_____

_____

_____

_____

What will you do this week to **develop**?

_____

_____

_____

_____

_____

_____

Who do you know that has made a positive **development**?

_____

_____

_____

_____

_____

_____

What positive things could come from **developing** as a person?

_____

_____

_____

_____

_____

_____

COURAGE

*"Be brave. You have to be willing to take the risk
to obtain your prize!"*

- Shennette Sparkes

How does this quote apply to your *life*?

_____

_____

_____

_____

_____

What will you do this week to show *courage*?

_____

_____

_____

_____

_____

Who do you know that shows *courage*?

_____

_____

_____

_____

_____

What positive things could come from having *courage*?

_____

_____

_____

_____

_____

DEDICATION

"Self-will so ardent and active that it will break a world to a piece to make a stool to sit on."

- Richard Cecil

How does this quote apply to your *life*?

_____

_____

_____

_____

_____

What will you do this week to show **dedication**?

_____

_____

_____

_____

_____

Who do you know that shows **dedication**?

_____

_____

_____

_____

_____

What positive things could come from showing **dedication**?

_____

_____

_____

_____

_____

WISDOM

"Reading is to the mind what exercise is to the body."
- Sir Richard Steele

How does this quote apply to your *life*?

_____
_____
_____
_____
_____
_____

What will you do this week to show **wisdom**?

_____
_____
_____
_____
_____
_____

Who do you know that is **wise**?

_____
_____
_____
_____
_____

What positive things could come from having **wisdom**?

_____
_____
_____
_____
_____

HOPE

"There is in this world no such force as a force of a person determined to rise. The human soul cannot be permanently changed."

- W.E.B. Du Bois

How does this quote apply to your *life*?

_____

_____

_____

_____

_____

What will you do this week to show *hope*?

_____

_____

_____

_____

_____

Who do you know that shows *hope*?

_____

_____

_____

_____

_____

What positive things could come from having *hope*?

_____

_____

_____

_____

_____

RESILIENCE

"No one can stop you, but you."

- Taj Williams

How does this quote apply to your *life*?

_____
_____
_____
_____
_____

What will you do this week to show *resilience*?

_____
_____
_____
_____
_____

Who do you know that shows *resilience*?

_____
_____
_____
_____
_____

What positive things could come from being *resilient*?

_____
_____
_____
_____
_____

ATTITUDE

"Pride is a personal commitment. It is an attitude which separates excellence from mediocrity."

- Unknown

How does this quote apply to your *life*?

_____
_____
_____
_____
_____
_____

What will you do this week to have a positive *attitude*?

_____
_____
_____
_____
_____
_____

Who do you know that has a positive *attitude*?

_____
_____
_____
_____
_____
_____

What positive things could come from having a positive *attitude*?

_____
_____
_____
_____
_____
_____

PERSISTENCE

"It's not whether you get knocked down, it's whether you get up."

- Vince Lombardi

How does this quote apply to your *life*?

_____

_____

_____

_____

_____

_____

What will you do this week to show **persistence**?

_____

_____

_____

_____

_____

_____

Who do you know that shows **persistence**?

_____

_____

_____

_____

_____

_____

What positive things could come from showing **persistence**?

_____

_____

_____

_____

_____

_____

SELF-DISCIPLINE

"We are what we repeatedly do. Excellence, therefore is not an act but a habit."

- Aristotle

How does this quote apply to your *life*?

_____
_____
_____
_____
_____
_____

What will you do this week to show *self-discipline*?

_____
_____
_____
_____
_____
_____

Who do you know that shows *self-discipline*?

_____
_____
_____
_____
_____
_____

What positive things could come from showing *self-discipline*?

_____
_____
_____
_____
_____
_____

MENTAL TOUGHNESS

"What didn't kill me, makes me stronger and wiser."
- Shennette Sparkes

How does this quote apply to your *life*?

_____
_____
_____
_____
_____
_____

What will you do this week to show *mental toughness*?

_____
_____
_____
_____
_____
_____

Who do you know that shows *mental toughness*?

_____
_____
_____
_____
_____
_____

What positive things could come from showing *mental toughness*?

_____
_____
_____
_____
_____
_____

ENDURANCE

"You measure the size of the accomplishment by the obstacles you had to overcome to reach your goals."
- Booker T. Washington

How does this quote apply to your *life*?

_____
_____
_____
_____
_____
_____

What will you do this week to show *endurance*?

_____
_____
_____
_____
_____
_____

Who do you know that shows *endurance*?

_____
_____
_____
_____
_____
_____

What positive things could come from showing *endurance*?

_____
_____
_____
_____
_____
_____

FOCUS

"Follow one course until successful."
- Amy Dobrikova

How does this quote apply to your *life*?

_____
_____
_____
_____
_____

What will you do this week to show *focus*?

_____
_____
_____
_____
_____

Who do you know that shows *focus*?

_____
_____
_____
_____
_____

What positive things could come from showing *focus*?

_____
_____
_____
_____
_____

PEACE

"Peace cannot be kept by force, it can only be achieved by understanding."

- Albert Einstein

How does this quote apply to your *life*?

_____
_____
_____
_____
_____
_____

What will you do this week to find *peace*?

_____
_____
_____
_____
_____
_____

Who do you know that is at *peace*?

_____
_____
_____
_____
_____
_____

What positive things could come from finding *peace*?

_____
_____
_____
_____
_____
_____

FAITH

"Life is what you make it."

- Unknown

How does this quote apply to your *life*?

_____
_____
_____
_____
_____
_____

What will you do this week to show *faith*?

_____
_____
_____
_____
_____
_____

Who do you know that has *faith*?

_____
_____
_____
_____
_____
_____

What positive things could come from having *faith*?

_____
_____
_____
_____
_____
_____

PURPOSE

"I've learned that people will forget what you said, people will forget what you did, but people will never forget how you made them feel."

- Maya Angelou

How does this quote apply to your *life*?

_____
_____
_____
_____
_____
_____

What will you do this week to fulfill your *purpose*?

_____
_____
_____
_____
_____
_____

Who do you know that shows *purpose*?

_____
_____
_____
_____
_____
_____

What positive things could come from following your *purpose*?

_____
_____
_____
_____
_____

CHANGE

"Today isn't about how we can improve our yesterdays, but how we can help direct our tomorrows."
- Shennette Sparkes

How does this quote apply to your *life*?

_____
_____
_____
_____
_____
_____

What will you do this week to make a *change*?

_____
_____
_____
_____
_____
_____

Who do you know that has made a positive *change*?

_____
_____
_____
_____
_____
_____

What positive things could come from making a *change*?

_____
_____
_____
_____
_____
_____

SELF-CONFIDENCE

"Confidence isn't about others view of you, rather about how you truly view yourself."

- Shennette Sparkes

How does this quote apply to your *life*?

_____

_____

_____

_____

_____

What will you do this week to show *self-confidence*?

_____

_____

_____

_____

_____

Who do you know that has *self-confidence*?

_____

_____

_____

_____

_____

What positive things could come from having *self-confidence*?

_____

_____

_____

_____

_____

PERSONAL DEVELOPMENT

"Age makes someone an adult, but maturity is what
makes someone a grown up"
- Shennette Sparkes

How does this quote apply to your *life*?

_____
_____
_____
_____
_____

What will you do this week to **develop**?

_____
_____
_____
_____
_____

Who do you know that has made a positive **development**?

_____
_____
_____
_____
_____

What positive things could come from **developing** as a person?

_____
_____
_____
_____
_____

COURAGE

"You miss 100% of the shots you do not take."
- Wayne Gretzky

How does this quote apply to your *life*?

_____
_____
_____
_____
_____
_____

What will you do this week to show *courage*?

_____
_____
_____
_____
_____
_____

Who do you know that shows *courage*?

_____
_____
_____
_____
_____

What positive things could come from having *courage*?

_____
_____
_____
_____
_____

DEDICATION

*"Every Champion was once a contender
that refused to give up."*

- Rocky Balboa

How does this quote apply to your *life*?

_____
_____
_____
_____
_____

What will you do this week to show **dedication**?

_____
_____
_____
_____
_____

Who do you know that shows **dedication**?

_____
_____
_____
_____
_____

What positive things could come from showing **dedication**?

_____
_____
_____
_____
_____

WISDOM

"The person without a purpose is like a ship without a rudder."

- Thomas Carlyle

How does this quote apply to your *life*?

_____
_____
_____
_____
_____
_____
_____

What will you do this week to show **wisdom**?

_____
_____
_____
_____
_____
_____
_____

Who do you know that is **wise**?

_____
_____
_____
_____
_____
_____
_____

What positive things could come from having **wisdom**?

_____
_____
_____
_____
_____
_____

HOPE

"We are a product of the choices we make, not the circumstances that we face."

- Roger Crawford

How does this quote apply to your *life*?

_____
_____
_____
_____
_____
_____

What will you do this week to show *hope*?

_____
_____
_____
_____
_____
_____

Who do you know that shows *hope*?

_____
_____
_____
_____
_____
_____

What positive things could come from having *hope*?

_____
_____
_____
_____
_____

RESILIENCE

"If you are scared, keep going: if you are hungry, keep going:
if you want to taste freedom, keep going."
- Harriet Tubman

How does this quote apply to your *life*?

_____
_____
_____
_____
_____
_____

What will you do this week to show *resilience*?

_____
_____
_____
_____
_____
_____

Who do you know that shows *resilience*?

_____
_____
_____
_____
_____
_____

What positive things could come from being *resilient*?

_____
_____
_____
_____
_____
_____

ATTITUDE

"Whether you think you can or think you can't, you're right!"
- Henry Ford

How does this quote apply to your *life*?

_____

_____

_____

_____

_____

What will you do this week to have a positive **attitude**?

_____

_____

_____

_____

_____

Who do you know that has a positive **attitude**?

_____

_____

_____

_____

_____

What positive things could come from having a positive **attitude**?

_____

_____

_____

_____

_____

PERSISTENCE

"Obstacles don't have to stop you. If you run into a wall, don't turn around and give up. Figure out how to climb it, go through it, or work around it."

- Michael Jordan

How does this quote apply to your *life*?

_____

_____

_____

_____

_____

_____

What will you do this week to show *persistence*?

_____

_____

_____

_____

_____

_____

Who do you know that shows *persistence*?

_____

_____

_____

_____

_____

_____

What positive things could come from showing *persistence*?

_____

_____

_____

_____

_____

_____

NOTES

NOTES

NOTES

NOTES

NOTES

NOTES

NOTES

NOTES

NOTES

NOTES

NOTES

www.ingramcontent.com/pod-product-compliance
Lightning Source LLC
LaVergne TN
LVHW041236080426
835508LV00011B/1231